D1085449

DATE DUE

The Hindenburg 1937:

A Huge Airship Destroyed by Fire

JANE BINGHAM

Raintree

CHICAGO, ILLINOIS

Designed by Victoria Bevan and AMR Design Ltd
Illustrations by David Woodroffe
Printed and bound in China by South China Printing
   Company

10 09 08 07 06
10 9 8 7 6 5 4 3 2 1

Library of Congress Cataloging-in-Publication Data
Bingham, Jane.
   The Hindenburg 1937 : a huge airship is destroyed
by fire / Jane
Bingham.
      p. cm. -- (When disaster struck)
   Includes bibliographical references and index.
   ISBN 1-4109-2281-2 (9781410922816)
   1. Hindenburg (Airship)--Juvenile literature. 2.
Aircraft accidents--New
Jersey--Juvenile literature. 3. Airships--Germany--
Juvenile literature. I.
Title. II. Series.

   TL659.H5B56 2006
   363.12'465--dc22
                           2005034864

Acknowledgments
The publishers would like to thank the following for
permission to reproduce photographs:
AKG Images p.31; Alamy Images p.4 (Popperfoto);
Corbis pp.10 (Bettmann), 13 (Bettmann),
14 (Hulton-Deutsch Collection), 16 (Austrian
Archives), 18 (Bettmann), 20 (Bettmann),
21 (Hulton-Deutsch Collection), 22, 26, 27, 32
(Bettmann), 36, 37 (Bettmann), 40 (Bettmann),
44 bottom (Bettmann), 49 (Reuters); Getty
Images pp.8 (Hulton Archive), 12 (Hulton Archive),
17 (Hulton Archive), 28 (Hulton Archive),
29 (Hulton Archive), 35 (Hulton Archive), 38
(Time & Life Pictures), 42 (Hulton Archive), 44 top
(Hulton Archive); Mary Evans Picture Library p.6;
The Advertising Archives p.19; The Kobal Collecton
p.46 (Universal).

Cover photograph of the *Hindenburg* in flames at
Lakeside, New Jersey, reproduced with permission
of Corbis (Bettmann Archive).

The publishers would like to thank Rick Zitarosa for
his assistance in the preparation of this book.

Every effort has been made to contact copyright
holders of any material reproduced in this book.
Any omissions will be rectified in subsequent
printings if notice is given to the publishers.

The paper used to print this book comes from
sustainable resources.

CONTENTS

Any words appearing in the text in bold, **like this**, are explained in the glossary.

A HUGE AIRSHIP DESTROYED BY FIRE

The *Hindenburg*, 1937

BREAKING NEWS

It was May 6, 1937. The crowd on the airfield had been waiting for hours for the *Hindenburg* to arrive.

The giant airship circled overhead, its captain waiting for a break in the heavy clouds. At long last, someone spotted a glint of silver. Everyone gazed in wonder as the magnificent airship approached the landing field.

Radio reporter Herb Morrison picked up his microphone, saying, "Here it comes, ladies and gentlemen. And what a sight it is. A thrilling one."

He was an expert reporter, and his description continued smoothly. But suddenly, his voice changed completely as he said, "It's burst into flames [...] oh my, this is terrible [...] It's burning, bursting into flames."

Morrison struggled on a little longer. Then, he broke down in tears. "Oh! I can't talk, ladies and gentlemen. I'm sorry," he said.

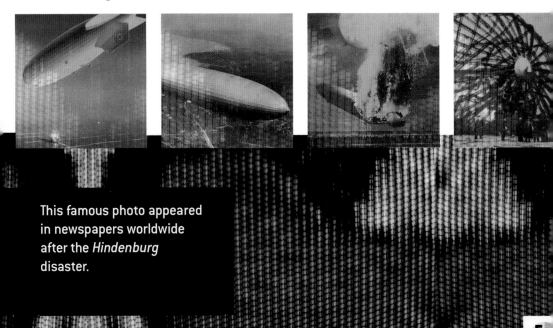

This famous photo appeared in newspapers worldwide after the *Hindenburg* disaster.

DR. ECKENER'S
DREAM

The *Hindenburg*, 1937

A PASSENGER AIRSHIP

By 1930 Dr. Hugo Eckener was head of the German Zeppelin Company, maker of the world's finest airships.

He was also a brilliant pilot. In 1929 Eckener had flown his airship, the *Graf Zeppelin*, around the world. This record-breaking flight made him an international hero. But now he had a new dream.

Dr. Eckener planned to build a new airship even larger and lighter than the *Graf Zeppelin*. The new airship would carry 50 passengers. This would make Germany a world leader in building passenger and **freight** airships. Eckener hoped that his beautiful airship would **inspire** everyone who saw it.

In 1930 Dr. Eckener's perfect airship was only a dream. Six years later, it became the *Hindenburg*.

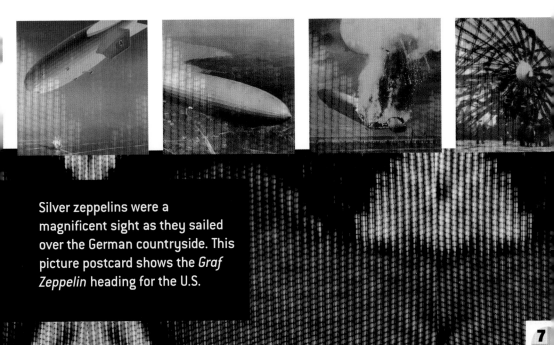

Silver zeppelins were a magnificent sight as they sailed over the German countryside. This picture postcard shows the *Graf Zeppelin* heading for the U.S.

BUILDING THE DREAM MACHINE

In 1931 work began on Dr. Eckener's dream machine. The first task was to build a shed large enough to house the biggest aircraft ever made.

Engineers constructed a huge metal **frame** made from lightweight supporting beams held together by thin wire braces. This **rigid** frame was extremely light, but also very strong.

A huge outer cover was then stretched tightly over the airship's metal frame. The cover was made from hundreds of strips of cotton tied to the supporting beams by cord.

The criss-cross construction of the metal frame made the *Hindenburg* more stable.

Once the airship's cover was in place, it was painted with several layers of **aluminium** paint. This metal coating reflected the rays of the Sun. This was intended as a safety device that would prevent the gas inside from becoming dangerously hot. The silver paint also gave the airship a shimmering, almost magical appearance.

Inside the massive body of the *Hindenburg* were sixteen cotton **cells**. Each of these cells was filled with **hydrogen** gas to make the airship float (see page 12). Below these cells, at the base of the ship, were large storage tanks. Some of the tanks held oil and diesel fuel for the engines. There were also several water tanks. These acted as **ballast** to weigh the airship down. In an emergency, water could be emptied out of the tanks to make the airship lighter. This would prevent it from sinking too fast and possibly crashing.

At the base of the airship were comfortable passenger **quarters**, arranged on two decks (see pp 24–25). The crew's living quarters were behind the passenger decks. The ship's officers had their own **accommodation** at the front of the airship. There was also a freight room used for storing heavy goods, a mail room, and a radio room.

The *Hindenburg* is still the largest aircraft that has ever flown. It measured 800 feet (244 meters) long. That is almost as long as the ocean liner *Titanic*! At its deepest point, it was as high as a thirteen-story building. The gas cells were filled with 7 million cubic feet (198,220 cubic meters) of hydrogen. That is almost the same volume as 80 Olympic swimming pools.

AIRSHIP OR SHIP?

Number of passengers:
Hindenburg: 50–70
Steamship: 2,000

Number of crew:
Hindenburg: 40–45
Steamship: 300

Time to cross the Atlantic:
Hindenburg: 2 to 2.5 days
Express steamship: 4 days

Price:
Hindenburg: Roughly the same as a first-class steamship ticket, but the price was subsidized by the German government.

Comfort:
Hindenburg: It was a smooth journey, but not as luxurious as first-class steamship travel.
Steamship: Many people became seasick.

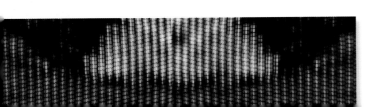

COMMANDING THE AIRSHIP

The massive *Hindenburg* was powered by four engines housed under the airship. Each engine turned a large **propeller**. Even if one engine failed, the airship's engineers were confident that the other three would continue to run. However, they were proved wrong on the *Hindenburg's* first major trip (see page 18).

The *Hindenburg* was kept on course by four large flaps attached to the four **fins** at the back of the airship. The upper and lower fins had **rudder** flaps that changed the airship's direction to the left or right. The two side fins had **elevator flaps** that controlled the angle, up or down, that the airship took through the sky.

In 1925 the U.S. airship *Shenandoah* ran into a violent storm. The airship was forced upward by the wind. Then it was caught on the side by a powerful gust and smashed to pieces.

At the front of the airship was a small **control car**. This hung below the airship, just in front of the passenger decks. The *Hindenburg's* control car had windows on all sides. The windows provided an excellent view of any obstacles and allowed the crew to keep a constant check on the weather.

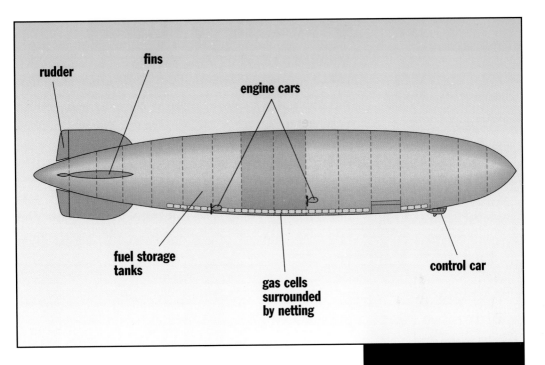

rudder

fins

engine cars

fuel storage
tanks

gas cells
surrounded
by netting

control car

From the *Hindenburg's* small control car, the captain and his officers commanded the airship. They changed the ship's direction by moving the rudders and the elevator flaps. They made the *Hindenburg* go faster or slower by controlling the power of its engines. The crew controlled the airship's height by adjusting the amount of hydrogen in the gas cells. It was done by releasing some hydrogen into the air. This was very dangerous and could not be done in a thunderstorm.

This is the internal design of the *Hindenburg*. It had a Mercedes engine.

There was a large set of **dials** and instruments to help the captain. These instruments showed the wind's speed and direction as well as the temperature outside the airship. The crew also received constant reports from the radio operator on the weather conditions ahead.

The captain's job required him to be highly skilled, but his duties were usually **routine**. However, the massive airship was always at the mercy of the weather. A **freak** storm could suddenly turn the captain's job into a desperate fight to prevent an accident.

HYDROGEN OR HELIUM?

Once the *Hindenburg* was ready to fly, its sixteen gas cells were filled with hydrogen. However, this was not the gas Dr. Eckener had wanted to use. He had planned to have his dream airship lifted by **helium**, a much safer gas than hydrogen.

All the early airships used hydrogen gas. Hydrogen is much lighter than air, so it gave excellent lift. It was also cheap to produce. In the 1920s, 1,000 cubic feet (28 cubic meters) of hydrogen could be bought for a couple of dollars. However, hydrogen has one serious drawback. When it mixes with air, it becomes very dangerous. The moment it then makes contact with a spark of fire, it bursts into flame.

Hydrogen was a serious safety **hazard** for airships. The airships were powered by sparking engines that could easily start a fire. Cooking ovens and passengers' smoking areas could also cause fires.

In 1922 the U.S. Army airship the *Roma* was forced to make a sudden landing because of bad weather. On its way down, it hit electricity wires. It exploded, and 33 of the 44 men on board were killed. After this, hydrogen was never used in a U.S. airship.

In the early 1920s, several airships ended up in flames. People were worried, so airship designers looked for a safer gas. In the United States, they decided to use helium. Helium cannot burn, but it has some disadvantages. It is not as light as hydrogen, so more gas is needed to lift the same load. It is also very expensive. In the 1920s, helium was only produced in Texas, and it was 50 times more expensive than hydrogen.

In spite of the cost, Eckener wanted to play it safe. He ordered that the *Hindenburg* be built large enough to carry helium gas. However, there was a problem with the supply. After World War I (1914–18), a law was passed in the United States. No helium could be sold to foreign countries. Everyone expected the law to be relaxed, but in 1936 the ban was still in place.

Eventually Eckener decided that his dream airship would use hydrogen. After all, this was the gas that German airships had used in the past, and they had an excellent safety record. Eckener thought that poor design had resulted in the other airships exploding. But using hydrogen was a decision he came to regret.

Dr. Hugo Eckener is shown at the controls of his dream ship. Dr. Eckener was a tall, impressive man who was very popular in Germany.

NAZI
PRIDE

The *Hindenburg, 1937*

THE NAZIS GAIN POWER

While the *Hindenburg* was being constructed, a new political party was gaining power under the leadership of Adolf Hitler.

The party was known as the National Socialist German Workers Party, or the Nazi party for short. Its members often relied on violence to get their way.

In 1933 President Paul von Hindenburg appointed Hitler as the chief minister in the German government. Hindenburg believed he could keep Hitler under control, but he was wrong. Within two years, Hitler and his Nazis were ruling Germany.

By the time Hitler seized power in Germany, the Zeppelin Company was short of money. Dr. Eckener did not like the Nazis, but he needed money to finish his airship.

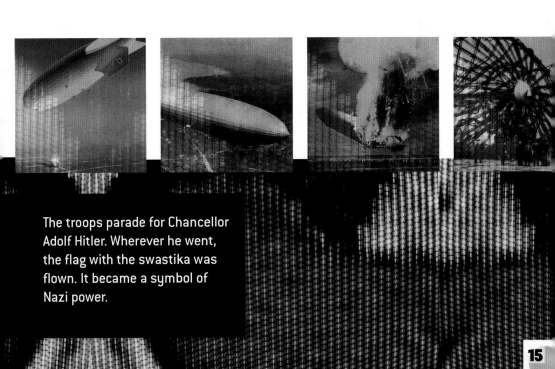

The troops parade for Chancellor Adolf Hitler. Wherever he went, the flag with the swastika was flown. It became a symbol of Nazi power.

THE PROPAGANDA FLIGHT

Hitler's **propaganda** minister, Dr. Joseph Goebbels, decided the new airship could be very useful to the Nazi party. He dreamed of the airship traveling around the world, showing what a great country Germany had become.

Goebbels announced that he would help fund Eckener's project. He ordered that the airship be decorated with the Nazi symbol, the swastika, which was the badge of the Nazi party. Wherever it traveled, the airship would be seen as a sign of Nazi success.

Hermann Göring, Hitler's air transportation minister, also promised lots of money to help build the new airship. He set up a zeppelin company controlled by the Nazi government that would oversee all of Dr. Eckener's work. Göring chose a young pilot named Ernst Lehmann to be head of the new company. Now it was Lehmann, not Eckener, who made the important decisions.

By March 1936, Eckener's dream airship was almost ready to fly, but it still had no name. Until that time, it was simply known as the LZ129. Some in the government wanted it named after Hitler. Hitler was worried that if the airship crashed, it would be seen as a bad sign for him. Hitler's government ordered that it be named the *Hindenburg*, after Paul von Hindenburg.

Preparations began for the airship's first major flight. It was going to fly to South America at the end of March, but first it needed some final tests. Eckener had planned careful safety checks, but the Nazis had other plans. They took control of the airship, and the checks were not completed.

The Nazis were using the *Hindenburg* to show their power, but Dr. Eckener had very different hopes for it. He described it as a "symbol of the universal dream of lasting peace among peoples."

Dr. Joseph Goebbels is shown (left) beside Adolf Hitler. Goebbels was Hitler's propaganda minister. His job was to promote Nazi ideas throughout Germany.

On March 26, 1936, Captain Ernst Lehmann took off on a special flight on the orders of Dr. Goebbels. The aim of the flight was to travel around Germany and drop propaganda leaflets for the Nazi party. As the airship took off, a powerful wind ripped a large tear in its back fin. Lehmann organized a quick repair, and the flight was made according to Goebbels's plan.

When Dr. Eckener found out what had happened to his airship, he was furious. It had not had the safety tests and had been damaged. Eckener told Lehmann he was a fool to try to please Goebbels. After this, many people feared what would happen to Dr. Eckener. Nobody criticized the Nazis and got away with it.

THE SWASTIKA

The symbol of the swastika is over 3,000 years old. It appears in the art of many civilizations, including ancient Greece, India, and China. For these ancient peoples, the swastika represented life, sun, power, strength, and good luck. Since the Nazis used the symbol, it has gained many negative meanings.

THE FIRST YEAR OF FLIGHT

On March 30, 1936, the *Hindenburg* set off as planned for Brazil. Because of Dr. Goebbels's propaganda flight, there had been no time to finish the safety checks. Dr. Eckener was worried that problems might develop during the flight. He was right.

On the flight to South America, one of the airship's four engines failed. When the *Hindenburg* arrived in Rio de Janeiro, the airship's engineers did their best to fix the damaged engine. However, they were only able to make it work at half speed. On the return trip, another engine failed. The *Hindenburg* struggled back to Germany using only two and a half engines.

Captain Ernst Lehmann waves from the control car of the *Hindenburg* in 1936.

Failing engines were not the only problem on the *Hindenburg*'s South American flight. While the airship was on its way to Rio, Goebbels heard about Eckener's criticism of him. When Eckener arrived in Rio, he learned that he had been pronounced a "**non-person**." He was no longer welcome in Germany.

For a while, it seemed as if Germany's hero of the air would not be able to live in his home country. But Dr. Eckener was persuaded to issue a public statement. He explained that he had only criticized Goebbels's plans because he feared for the airship's safety. Goebbels announced that he was satisfied with this explanation. Eckener was allowed to prepare for the *Hindenburg's* busy schedule ahead.

The *Hindenburg's* trip to Rio was the first of many international flights. In May the airship left for New York. This was a remarkably smooth and successful trip. It was the start of a busy **season** of flights. By the end of 1936, the *Hindenburg* had completed ten round trips from Germany to New York and seven to Rio. During all these trips, the airship experienced no serious engine trouble. It carried many rich and famous passengers who thoroughly enjoyed the experience.

IN 2 DAYS ACROSS THE ATLANTIC
DEUTSCHE ZEPPELIN-REEDEREI
HAMBURG-AMERIKA LINIE

A German poster advertises the *Hindenburg*. For people rich enough to afford the fare, this was the fast and glamorous way to travel to New York.

MILLIONAIRES' FLIGHT

In 1936 Dr. Eckener invited as his personal guests 72 of the most powerful men in the U.S. They were taken on a ten-hour round trip over New York and the New England countryside. They ate a lavish dinner and enjoyed beautiful views. The "millionaires' flight" was given much publicity. The *Hindenburg's* first year ended in triumph.

AT THE OLYMPIC GAMES

Hitler was delighted with the *Hindenburg's* success, but he had other plans for the new airship. In August 1936 Germany hosted the Olympic Games. The Nazis saw this as a chance to show off their power.

At the Olympic Games' opening ceremony, Nazi flags and uniforms were everywhere. Floating above the stadium were the two massive German airships, the *Graf Zeppelin* and the *Hindenburg*. Painted on the airships' sides was the Olympic symbol of the five linked rings. But this peaceful symbol was dwarfed by the enormous swastika badges on their tail fins.

The Nazis used the *Hindenburg* to demonstrate their power.

A German zeppelin hovers over a harbor just before the start of World War I.

Every year the Nazi party held a political rally in Nuremberg, Germany. Troops marched through the city and people flocked to hear Hitler and other Nazi leaders speak. The rally was meant to show off Nazi power. The *Hindenburg* was also present at Nuremberg in September 1936. By then it was clear that Hitler had won the loyalty of many Germans. This made people all over the world very worried.

The sight of a zeppelin in the sky at Nuremberg added to the world's fear. The German zeppelins had caused terrible destruction in World War I. Although the zeppelins had not been a lasting weapon, the sight of a German airship brought back frightening memories. It also sent out a clear message: the Nazis had the power to dominate the skies.

DANGER FROM THE SKIES

In 1915, a year after World War I began, German zeppelins flew along the coast checking out British defenses. Others arrived in the dead of night to drop firebombs on British cities. The silent bombers caused much death and destruction. At first, the British were not able to defend themselves. However, with better planes and bullets, British pilots soon learned how to shoot them down. By 1917 the German zeppelin bombing raids had ended.

CROSSING THE ATLANTIC

ATLANTIC

The *Hindenburg*, 1937

A FLYING HOTEL

In 1937 the early excitement about the Hindenburg began to fade.

Meanwhile many Germans chose to stay at home. They were worried about their families in the growing atmosphere of violence. Germany was making enemies abroad, and people feared that the *Hindenburg* might be a target for a bomb attack.

For all these reasons, the *Hindenburg* was only half full when it set off for the United States on the first **transatlantic** flight of 1937.

Passengers on the *Hindenburg* traveled in style. All the rooms had been carefully designed to be stylish, comfortable, and safe. Much money was spent making their trip as enjoyable as possible.

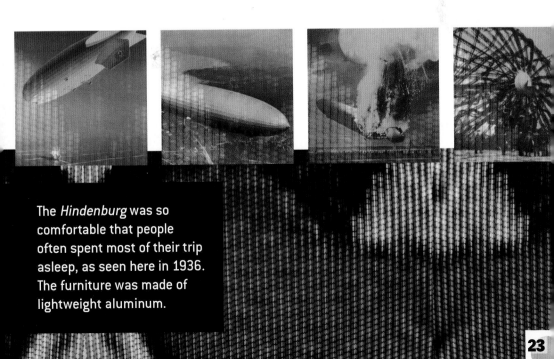

The *Hindenburg* was so comfortable that people often spent most of their trip asleep, as seen here in 1936. The furniture was made of lightweight aluminum.

DECK LAYOUTS

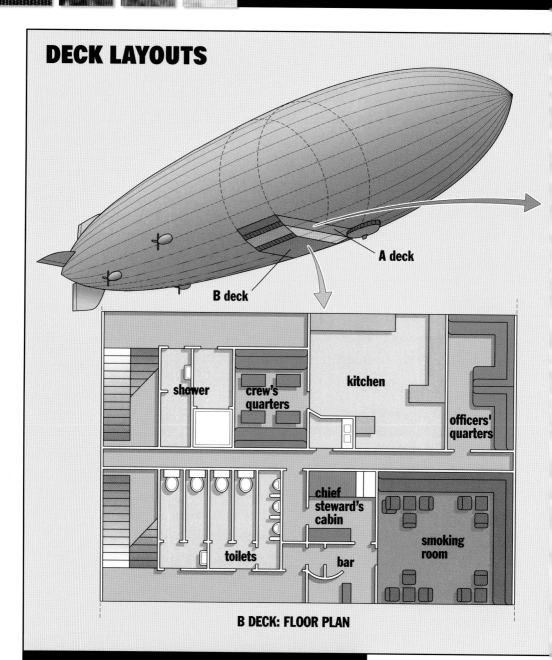

A deck

B deck

shower

crew's quarters

kitchen

officers' quarters

toilets

chief steward's cabin

bar

smoking room

B DECK: FLOOR PLAN

B DECK: FLOOR PLAN
There was a shower room, a small bar, and a smoking room. The smoking room had an airlock door. If a fire started, this door would prevent it from reaching the rest of the airship. This would reduce the risk of a spark coming into contact with the airship's hydrogen gas.

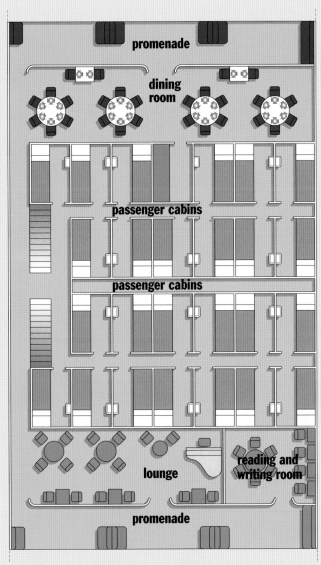

promenade

dining room

passenger cabins

passenger cabins

lounge

reading and writing room

promenade

A DECK: FLOOR PLAN

A DECK: FLOOR PLAN
In the center were 25 double cabins fitted with
bunk beds and a pantry. Both sides of A deck had
airy **promenades,** where passengers could walk
and look through huge windows that slanted
inward to give a lovely view of the land below.

LIFE ON BOARD THE AIRSHIP

Dining on board the *Hindenburg* was an unforgettable experience. The passengers sat at tables set with fine china that had been specially designed for the Zeppelin Company. On the walls of the dining room were paintings showing the voyages of the *Graf Zeppelin.* Meanwhile, passengers facing outward could enjoy a view of the changing skyline.

The passengers were joined each night by the captain and leading crew members. Helpful waiters dressed in neat uniforms served them. If the *Hindenburg* tipped by ten degrees, a wine glass would fall over. So, the crew were given strict orders to limit any ups and downs to five degrees while the passengers were eating meals. The food served on the *Hindenburg* was excellent.

Two passengers enjoy afternoon tea in the elegant dining room. The large, sloping windows allowed passengers to enjoy spectacular views.

The airship had an expert chef. Passengers could choose from **delicacies** such as fattened duckling with champagne cabbage or **venison** cutlets. All the dishes were freshly prepared and cooked in a large kitchen.

Each meal was freshly cooked. Here, a chef prepares dinner in the *Graf Zeppelin's* kitchen.

The kitchen had an electric stove, ovens, a refrigerator, and an ice machine. The kitchen was directly below the dining room. The dishes were sent straight up in an elevator known as a dumbwaiter. The waiters would then take them piping hot to the passengers' tables.

The Zeppelin Company made sure its passengers were never bored. There were books to borrow from the library, chessboards to use, and special cards and writing paper for sending messages home. The passengers' mail was stamped in the mailroom with the *Hindenburg's* special stamp.

There were guided tours of the *Hindenburg* and, for the adventurous, an outdoor walk to one of the airship's engine cars. The ship's doctor provided his services free of charge. A priest even held church services.

Everyone seemed to have a good time aboard the *Hindenburg*. The only disadvantage was the price. A one-way trip to New York cost as much as a car. Only the very rich could afford it.

STOCKING UP

Apart from dinner each evening, passengers were also served breakfast, lunch, and afternoon tea. A typical Atlantic crossing lasted three days. In this time, the chef used 440 pounds (200 kilograms) of fresh meat and 800 eggs.

THE BUSY CREW

When the *Hindenburg* set off for New York on May 3, 1937, it was carrying 97 people. There were 36 passengers and a crew of 40. There were also 21 extra Zeppelin Company employees. These included Dr. Rudiger, the in-flight doctor, and a few young airshipmen in training. Two dogs were traveling in special cabins at the back of the airship.

Captain Max Pruss was commanding the airship. He was an expert airship pilot who had recently taken over from Ernst Lehmann as captain of the *Hindenburg*.

Lehmann was now busy running the Zeppelin Company, but he joined the trip as an **observer**. In addition to Pruss and Lehmann, there was a second observer and a first and second officer. This meant there were five experienced pilots on board.

A SHADOW OF SADNESS

Dr. Hugo Eckener had been an honored passenger on many of the *Hindenburg's* earlier trips. But this time, he was on a lecture tour. It was left to Captain Lehmann to socialize with the passengers, spreading the company's message of confidence in their airship. Unfortunately, Lehmann was not in his usual good spirits. The previous month his only son had died from pneumonia (a lung infection). Lehmann was quiet and withdrawn.

A smiling Ernst Lehmann (front right) stands beside Dr. Eckener (center) in 1928. In May 1937, however, Lehmann was not happy. His only son had just died.

By 1937 the *Hindenburg* crew members all knew their jobs perfectly. All the measuring instruments in the control car had to be checked constantly. A careful **log** was kept of the *Hindenburg's* progress.

The mechanics maintained all the equipment in perfect order. They made regular inspections of the metal frame. They also kept a constant check on the engines and the cells containing hydrogen gas. One of the toughest jobs was engine duty. The mechanics had to take turns standing inside the engine cars, making sure the propellers and engines were working properly. Apart from the deafening noise, the heat could become unbearable. It reached over 113°F (45 °C) when flying over the **tropics**.

The kitchen staff was kept very busy preparing and cooking meals for the passengers and crew. Well-trained stewards looked after all the passengers' needs. All the stewards had been male on the *Hindenburg's* previous trips. For the 1937 season, they were joined by Emilie Imhof, the first airship stewardess.

A member of the crew is shown at the *Hindenburg's* steering wheel before a flight. All the equipment was checked constantly to make sure it was safe.

THE AIRSHIP'S PASSENGERS

The passengers on board the *Hindenburg* came from different backgrounds. Some were very wealthy individuals who were used to transatlantic travel. Some were families visiting their relatives in the United States. A few were journalists traveling free of charge. Others were returning home to the United States after working in Europe.

Among them was Margaret Mather. She was a 59-year-old American who lived in Rome, but often visited New York. It was her first voyage in an airship, and she kept a detailed record of her trip.

At 8:00 P.M. on May 3, the *Hindenburg* took off in perfect weather. It headed north across the Atlantic Ocean past the southern tip of Greenland. Once out at sea, it was slowed down by powerful winds of up to 50 miles (80.5 kilometers) per hour. Everyone was amazed at how steadily the *Hindenburg* stayed on course.

TOY TRUCK ALERT

In her detailed description of life on board, Margaret Mather described two brothers. Walter was eight years old and Werner was six. The boys liked to play with their toys in the lounge. Mather was very impressed by their manners. They did not even make a fuss when a steward took away Werner's metal truck because its clockwork motor made tiny sparks.

This is the route the *Hindenburg* took from Germany to New York.

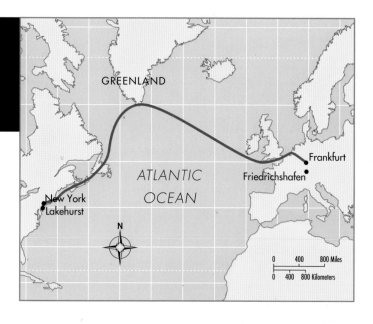

Passengers enjoy the view from the promenade deck on a flight in 1936. Very few images survive from the fatal flight of 1937.

Margaret Mather was especially delighted by the smoothness of the flight. She had suffered terrible seasickness on her previous Atlantic crossings by ship. Traveling by airship seemed the perfect answer.

For the next two days, the trip continued peacefully. Mather spent most of her time reading and writing in the comfortable lounge. She also strolled along the promenade, gazing out of the windows to catch a glimpse of the ocean below.

Unfortunately, the weather was gray and misty, so there was little to see. There was also a powerful wind that managed to slow down the *Hindenburg's* progress. However, time passed pleasantly enough. Nobody was worried that they would arrive in New York six hours later than planned.

THE JOURNEY'S END

The *Hindenburg, 1937*

SEEING LAND

On the morning of May 6, Margaret Mather woke up relaxed and cheerful.

The *Hindenburg* was now approaching the United States. Around noon she spotted Boston through the mist. "A great feeling of elation [happiness] seized me," she wrote later, "joy that I had flown—that I had crossed the sea with none of the usual weariness and distress."

By 3:00 P.M. the *Hindenburg* was over New York City. As they passed the Empire State Building, passengers on the *Hindenburg* waved to tourists on the skyscraper's observation deck. Then, the airship traveled south for a glimpse of the Statue of Liberty.

Half an hour after leaving New York, the *Hindenburg* arrived at Lakehurst, New Jersey. Lakehurst Station was where the *Hindenburg* would land.

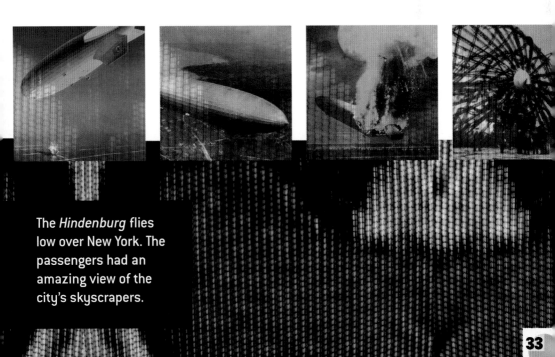

The *Hindenburg* flies low over New York. The passengers had an amazing view of the city's skyscrapers.

BAD WEATHER

While the *Hindenburg* was flying over New York, Captain Charles Rosendahl was getting worried. As commander of the Lakehurst Station, he had to decide whether conditions were safe for landing. All day long Rosendahl had been visiting the airfield's weather center to get the latest updates. The weather reports were not looking good. A line of thunderclouds was approaching Lakehurst.

Rosendahl knew that the *Hindenburg* was running very late. The airship was originally scheduled to land at six in the morning, but it was now mid-afternoon. Captain Pruss had sent a radio message announcing he would reach the airfield around 4:00 P.M. But Rosendahl could see from his weather reports that this was exactly the time that a massive storm cloud was due to arrive in the Lakehurst area.

At 4:00 P.M. the *Hindenburg* arrived at Lakehurst. Looking out of the windows, Margaret Mather noticed that no preparations had been made on the ground for landing. She also saw that the weather was getting worse.

Meanwhile, in the *Hindenburg's* control car, Captain Pruss had just received the latest weather report from Lakehurst. The report warned of powerful winds. Pruss also saw the ink-colored sky. These were obviously not the right conditions for landing. He radioed Rosendahl to say that he would fly toward the coast and wait for news from Lakehurst.

This slight delay did not worry the passengers very much. They were sure that they would soon be safely

LAST-MINUTE VISIT

One of the passengers was impatient to land. He was Joseph Späh, a comedian and acrobat who had worked in Europe for three months. Späh was very excited about seeing his children again because he had a special present for them. While he was in Germany, he had bought a dog named Ulla. He was eager to see his three little children's faces when he gave them their new pet. Ulla was kept in a kennel toward the back of the airship, but Späh insisted on feeding her himself. He took advantage of the delay to pay one more visit to Ulla in her special cabin.

on the ground. In the meantime, they enjoyed the spectacular views of the beaches of New Jersey.

At 5:00 P.M. Captain Rosendahl gave orders for **Zero Hour** to be sounded. A loud siren summoned the ground crew to get ready for the landing. By 6:00 P.M. everyone was in place. Rosendahl sent a radio message to Captain Pruss, saying, "Conditions now considered suitable for landing." However, it took two more messages before Pruss decided that it was safe to go back to Lakehurst.

At 7:10 P.M. Rosendahl radioed Pruss again, saying, "Conditions definitely improved recommend earliest possible landing." He ordered the ground crew to take up their final positions and hurried to join the waiting crowd on the airfield.

The *Hindenburg* flew over the New Jersey coast for two hours before Captain Pruss decided it was safe to land.

COMING IN TO LAND

Everyone was gathered around the mooring mast. This was a tall metal structure that the airship would be tied to once it had landed. When Rosendahl arrived, he heard people calling, "There she is!" Then, he looked up to see the huge, silver airship.

Up in the *Hindenburg's* control car, Captain Pruss prepared to land. He was in charge, but the two observers and the first and second officers were also in the control car. There was a light rain, but they were not worried. They had experienced dozens of landings before.

The enormous *Hindenburg* comes in to land at Lakehurst.

Pruss steered the *Hindenburg* in a large circle over the airfield, gradually releasing hydrogen gas to lower the airship. He made a sharp turn and approached the mooring mast. As he turned, the first officer noticed that the airship was heavy in the rear, so he adjusted its weight by letting out some water ballast from the **stern**.

On the ground, Captain Rosendahl watched calmly as the ship's heavy landing ropes were dropped. Everything seemed to be going according to plan. In a few minutes, the *Hindenburg* would be pulled slowly toward its mooring mast. Then, it would be fixed firmly in place and the passengers and crew would leave the airship. Rosendahl looked forward to welcoming his old friend, Captain Ernst Lehmann, again.

But then something totally unexpected happened. "I saw a burst of flame on top of the ship," Rosendahl later remembered. "It was a brilliant burst of flame resembling a flower opening rapidly into bloom. I knew at once that the airship was doomed."

Stunned spectators watch the disaster happening.

37

BLAZING INFERNO

For a few seconds, the burst of flame hung over the top of the airship. But nothing could stop the fire from reaching the hydrogen gas stored directly below. There was a muffled bang, and then flames swallowed up the back of the airship.

Flames and smoke shoot high into the air as the *Hindenburg* crashes, tail-first, to the ground.

The crowd on the airfield gasped out loud. Seconds before, they were taking photos and waving at the passengers in the airship. Now, they stared in horror as the field was lit by a white glow and as they felt the intense heat of the flames.

Meanwhile, in the front of the ship, the crew and passengers did not know what had happened. For some passengers, the first sign that anything was wrong was when they saw people on the ground pointing in horror at the airship. Then, they heard the terrifying thump of the explosion and saw the reflected glow of fire through the windows.

In the control car, Captain Pruss and his colleagues were just as shocked as their passengers. In spite of all their experience, there was nothing they could do to put out the fire. Once it took hold, flames raced along the length of the airship. Towering clouds of flame and smoke leapt high into the air. Then, the ship's stern sunk to the ground, breaking the *Hindenburg's* back.

Seconds after the stern hit the ground, a white-hot flame raced through the center of the airship. It traveled so fast that it shot out of the front like a huge firework. Then, the whole airship went up in flames.

TIMELINE

May 3, 1937 The *Hindenburg* **leaves Frankfurt, Germany.**

May 4–5 It crosses the Atlantic Ocean, slowed by strong winds.

May 6, 3:00 P.M. The *Hindenburg* **flies over New York City.**

4:00 P.M. The airship arrives at Lakehurst in stormy weather. Captain Pruss is told to delay landing and heads for the New Jersey coast.

6:00 P.M. Pruss is given the all-clear to land.

7:00 P.M. The *Hindenburg* **approaches the Lakehurst landing field.**

7:07 P.M. It makes a sharp turn.

7:16 P.M. The airship is heavy in the stern, so some water ballast is released.

7:21 P.M. The first mooring rope is dropped to the ground.

7:25 P.M. The rear of the *Hindenburg* **bursts into flames. Within 35 seconds, the whole airship is a blazing wreck.**

ESCAPING THE AIRSHIP

For many on board the *Hindenburg*, escape was impossible. Trapped inside their cabins, they burned to death immediately. But most managed to escape alive. Many threw themselves out of windows and were rushed to safety by the ground crew.

Joseph Späh, the acrobat, used his camera to smash one of the promenade windows. The front part of the *Hindenburg* was still too high to jump from. He dangled outside the promenade by one hand. Because of his gymnastic skills, he managed to hang on until it was safe to jump. Späh hobbled from the wreckage straight into the arms of his waiting family.

After jumping free from the ship, one of the stewards saw the young brothers, Walter and Werner, looking fearfully out of a window. Their mother pushed the boys out. The steward caught one of them. The other, with his hair on fire, fell at the steward's feet. Thankfully, they had no serious injuries. Both boys survived. Their mother was helped to safety, but their father died in the airship. Their sister Irene died from severe burns.

Shocked and injured passengers stumble from the wreckage and are helped to safety by people on the ground.

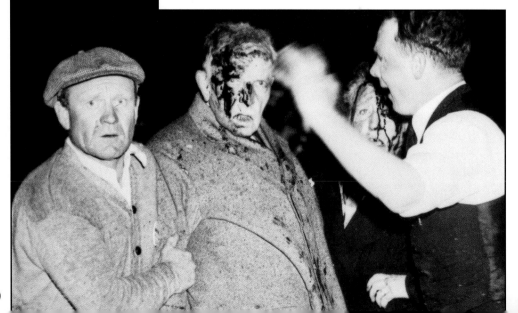

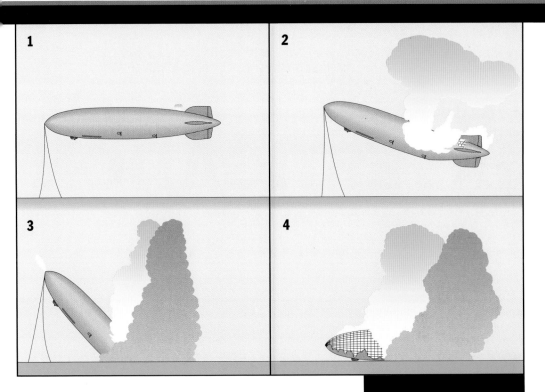

Some passengers escaped almost entirely unharmed. Margaret Mather did not try to leave the ship. She was still sitting inside the promenade deck when the burning *Hindenburg* hit the ground. The next thing she knew, some ground crew were waving to her from outside the airship. Captain Rosendahl reported, "As though led by a guardian angel she left the airship by the regular hatchway [...] receiving only minor burns."

Captain Pruss and the rest of the crew in the control car were all able to jump to safety, although most of them were very badly burned. Pruss was badly burned. His life was in serious danger for many days, but he survived. Captain Lehmann died later from his burns.

Miraculously, 23 passengers and 39 crew members survived. Of the people who were on board, 35 of the 97 died. One ground crew member also died.

In only 34 seconds, the *Hindenburg* was destroyed in a blazing fire.

THE CHILDREN GET A DOG

Ulla the dog died in the *Hindenburg*. The Alsation's full name was Ulla von Hooptel. Joseph Späh had used the pet in one of his acts on stage. On the drive home from Lakehurst, Späh told his oldest son, four-year-old Gilbert, that Ulla had miraculously survived. A few days later, the delighted children got a new dog.

THE INVESTIGATION

The *Hindenburg*, 1937

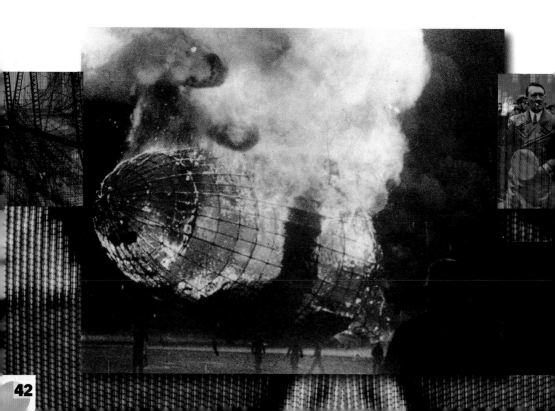

THE END OF A DREAM

Within days of the disaster, horrifying pictures of the blazing airship appeared in newspapers everywhere.

German zeppelins had an excellent safety record. If the *Hindenburg* could go up in flames, there was no future for airships, the newspaper editors said. Many had believed that airships were the future for long distance travel. The terrible crash marked the end of this hope.

The horror continued in the days after the crash. More victims died from their painful burns.

People began to ask difficult questions. What was the cause of the crash? Was there a problem in the design of the *Hindenburg*? Or, had someone planted a bomb in the airship as a deliberate protest against the Nazis?

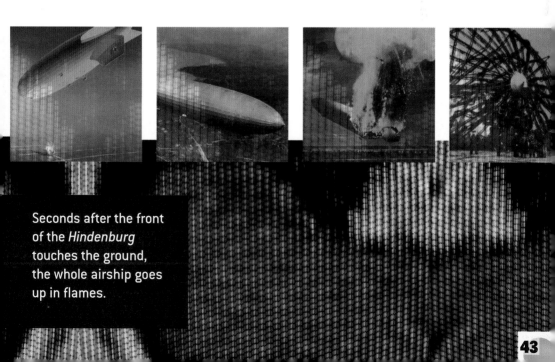

Seconds after the front of the *Hindenburg* touches the ground, the whole airship goes up in flames.

SEARCHING FOR EVIDENCE

ZEPPELIN BLAST KILLS THIRTY-FIVE

The day after the crash, newspapers all over the world showed the shocking images.

Within days, a team of experts gathered at Lakehurst to investigate the cause of the crash. One of the team leaders was Dr. Hugo Eckener. He had left for the United States on a ship as soon as he got the terrible news. He did not even have time to pack a toothbrush!

The team carried out a detailed inspection of what was left of the burned-out airship.

The team conducted many interviews. Surviving members of the crew were questioned closely. The team also interviewed people who had witnessed the crash from the ground.

In addition, there was film to look at. Never before had cameramen been present to record every second of a disaster. Although it was difficult to find the cause of the crash, there were a few clues.

The wreckage of the *Hindenburg* lies smoldering on the airfield at Lakehurst.

Some spectators had seen the first flash of flame at the rear of the airship. They had noticed that the outer covering in that area was fluttering loose in the breeze. Several crew members also reported that the *Hindenburg* was very heavy in the rear as it approached the landing field. On May 20 the experts gave their opinions at a **public inquiry** into the disaster.

Dr. Eckener believed that one of the gas cells had begun to leak just before the airship came in to land. The evidence for this leak was the fluttering cover and extra weight in the airship's rear. Eckener noted that Captain Pruss had made a sharp turn just before his final approach. He suggested that the strain of the turn had caused a supporting wire to snap. This wire made a hole in one of the hydrogen cells. Once hydrogen gas was leaking, it was only a matter of time before the gas met a spark of fire.

Inspectors view an engine. Parts of the wrecked airship were covered with fabric to preserve them for further inspections.

STATIC ELECTRICITY OR A BOMB?

The German scientist Max Dieckmann explained how sparks were created. He said that the recent thunderstorm had caused a difference in the **electrical charge** between the clouds above the airship and the ground below it.

Dieckmann believed that when the mooring ropes hit the ground, sparks of electricity traveled up the ropes. These caused the hydrogen gas to catch fire.

This is a still picture from the movie *The Hindenburg*. The movie explores the theory of a bomb.

Once all the experts had given their opinions, the **inquiry committee** gave its judgment. It said that the crash was the result of a tragic accident. The committee stated that the "most probable" cause of the disaster was a spark of **static electricity** that set fire to the hydrogen gas inside the cells.

As far as the public inquiry was concerned, that was the end of the matter. But many people believed the mystery was unsolved. They were convinced a bomb had caused the explosion.

Several of the passengers and crew were suspected of planting a bomb in the rear of the airship.

At first the acrobat Joseph Späh seemed the most likely secret bomber. His job as a touring entertainer looked like the perfect cover for a spy. He had also made several trips to the rear of the airship, apparently to visit his dog. Späh was investigated by detectives and thoroughly questioned before they decided he was innocent.

In the end, no evidence was found against any passenger, but one crew member has remained under suspicion. In the rear of the airship was a shy young man named Erich Spehl. He had a girlfriend who was suspected of plotting to destroy the Nazis. It is possible that Erich planted a bomb to please his girlfriend.

In 1962 a book was written blaming Spehl. Since then another book and a movie called *The Hindenburg* have repeated the same claim. Spehl died in the fire, so no one has been able to prove this theory.

A SUSPICIOUS PACKAGE

Joseph Späh aroused the suspicion of the Nazi Gestapo (secret police) before the *Hindenburg* even took off. In Germany he had been spotted in fancy restaurants with people who did not support Hitler. Späh never gave a straight answer. His practical-joker personality made the Nazi government suspicious. When Späh arrived to board the *Hindenburg*, he had a package wrapped in brown paper under his arm. He made inspectors angry by clowning around as they forced him to open it. All they found was a doll for his daughter.

AIRSHIPS AFTER HINDENBURG

At the time of the *Hindenburg* disaster, a new airship was being built in Germany. Most people thought that work on it would stop immediately. But air transportation minister Göring had other plans. He did not want the *Hindenburg* crash to make the Nazis look weak. So, Göring simply gave orders that German airships should be filled with helium gas.

In the end, the U.S. government refused to sell helium to the Nazis. The Germans were forced to use hydrogen for their airships. The new airship never carried any paying passengers. Two years later, all the German airships were deliberately destroyed. The metal parts from the airships were melted down to make aircraft bombers.

During World War II (1939–45), the U.S. Navy used non-rigid airships known as **blimps**. They had no metal frame. These small airships patrolled the oceans. Their crew kept a constant lookout for enemy submarines, ships, and planes. Blimps also escorted U.S. ships and warned their captains of any attacks. Blimps continued to be used after World War II, but by the 1950s they had largely disappeared.

Today, helium-filled airships are often used by companies to advertise their products. These colorful crafts have the company's name in giant letters on them. They are seen by thousands of people on the ground, often at sports events.

Some small airships also carry passengers on short sightseeing trips. The German Zeppelin Company has developed new small sightseeing airships. They take passengers on hour-long flights around the Swiss Alps. This is very popular with tourists.

There are exciting plans for airships in the future. The Japan Aerospace company has designed a huge unmanned airship that will hover 12.4 miles (20 kilometers) above Earth. If the Japanese plans go ahead, the airship will have electronic equipment for **broadcasting**. Its equipment will also **monitor** any changes in the surrounding weather conditions.

In Europe there are plans for a fleet of passenger airships. These ships would travel between ten major cities in Europe. Each of them would carry about 40 passengers and their luggage.

Whatever happens in the future, one thing is certain. People will never forget the lessons learned from the *Hindenburg*.

Today, airships are often used by companies for advertising. Here, an airship is used to promote the Olympics Games that were held in Athens, Greece.

TIMELINE

1783	The Montgolfier brothers test the world's first hydrogen balloon.
1852	Henri Giffard invents the **dirigible**, a steerable balloon with a steam engine.
1883	The Tissandier brothers construct a dirigible with a motor engine.
1906	Count Ferdinand von Zeppelin makes his first successful flight on the airship he invented. It has a rigid frame.
1908	The first U.S. airship is built.
1911	The British build their first rigid airship.
1922	The Italian-built *Roma* crashes in the United States. After that, U.S. airship designers use helium gas.
1925	The U.S. airship *Shenandoah* is destroyed in a storm.
1926	The Italian pilot Umberto Nobile flies the Norwegian airship, *Norge*, to the North Pole.
1929	Dr. Hugo Eckener flies the *Graf Zeppelin* around the world.
1930	The giant British airship, the *R101*, crashes on its first overseas flight. Forty-eight die and six survive.
1931	Work begins on the *Hindenburg*.
1933	The U.S. airship *Akron* crashes into the sea. Seventy-six die and three survive.
1935	The U.S. airship *Macon* crashes into the sea.

March 1936	The *Hindenburg* makes its first test flight.
March 31, 1936	The *Hindenburg* departs for Brazil on it first international flight.
May 1936	The *Hindenburg* travels from Germany to the United States on its first transatlantic flight.
May 3, 1937	The *Hindenburg* sets off for the United States, its first flight of the 1937 season.
May 6, 1937	The *Hindenburg* explodes as it comes in to land at Lakehurst, New Jersey.
May 10, 1937	A public inquiry is opened into the cause of the *Hindenburg* disaster.
1938	A new German zeppelin, *Graf Zeppelin II*, is launched. It never carries passengers.
1940	Field Marshall Hermann Göring gives orders for the Zeppelin Company construction sheds to be demolished. All German airships are broken up.
1950s	Blimps are used for military patrols and observation.
1980s	Blimps are used by companies to advertise their company name.
1990s	Research begins into a new generation of airships for transporting heavy equipment and even carrying passengers.

GLOSSARY

accommodation place where people can stay and sleep

aluminium strong, lightweight, silver-colored metal

ballast something heavy, such as water, carried by a ship or airship to make it more stable

blimp small airship that can be steered and is powered by an engine, but does not have a rigid frame

broadcast to send out sounds and pictures on television or radio

cell enclosed space that can be completely closed off

control car large cabin under an airship containing the equipment needed to control the airship

delicacies very special and expensive foods

dial circle of numbers that has a pointer from the center that moves around the numbers to show a measurement

dirigible air balloon, similar to an airship, that can be steered and has an engine to power it

electrical charge current of electricity that moves from one object to another

elevator flap moveable flap attached to an airship for steering it up or down

engineer someone who works with or designs engines and machines. Some engineers also design bridges and roads.

fin large structure at the top and the bottom of airships, like the fin of a fish, that helped airships remain stable in the air

frame structure around which something is built or made

freak sudden, unusual, or unexpected

freight goods or cargo carried by a vehicle or ship

hazard risk of harm or danger

helium lighter-than-air gas that does not catch fire easily

hydrogen lightest gas that exists. It catches fire easily.

inquiry committee group of people who have to find out the truth about something

inspire to encourage someone by giving him or her confidence and new ideas

log official record of what happens on a journey

monitor keep a constant check on

non-person someone who is no longer recognized by his or her country. The country might deny the person legal or social rights.

observer someone who watches something being done to make sure it is done properly

promenade broad pathway for people to walk along and enjoy the view

propaganda ideas or news spread by a party or group to persuade people to support them

propeller one of a set of turning blades that provides the force to move a vehicle through air or water

public inquiry investigation to find the truth about something and report it to the public

quarters rooms where people sleep and put their things

rigid stiff and impossible to bend

routine normal and not difficult or unusual

rudder movable flap attached to an airship or ship for steering it to the left or right

season period of time within one year when something usually happens

static electricity electricity caused by one surface rubbing against another

stern back of a ship or an airship

subsidize support or help by paying part of the money

transatlantic across the Atlantic Ocean, usually from the United States or Canada to Europe, or the other way around

tropics part of Earth's surface between the Tropic of Cancer and Tropic of Capricorn (imaginary lines near the middle of Earth) where it is very hot

venison meat from a deer or antelope

zero hour time for the start of an operation or action

FINDING OUT MORE

BOOKS

Botting, Douglas. *Dr. Eckener's Dream Machine: The Great Zeppelin and the Dawn of Air Travel*. New York: Henry Holt, 2001.

Dowswell, Paul. *Weapons and Technology of World War I*. Chicago: Heinemann Library, 2002.

Harris, Nathaniel. *The Rise of Hitler*. Chicago: Heinemann Library, 2004.

Saunders, Nigel. *Hydrogen*. Chicago: Heinemann Library, 2004.

Sherrow, Victoria. *The Hindenburg Disaster: Doomed Airship*. Berkeley Heights, N.J.: Enslow, 2002.

Townsend, John. *Outrageous Inventions.* Chicago: Raintree, 2006.

MOVIES

The Hindenburg (1975) starring George C. Scott and Anne Bancroft. This explores the theory that the airship was destroyed by a bomb. Parental guidance is advised.

Zeppelin (1971) starring Michael York and Elke Sommer. This tells the story of a double agent in a German World War I zeppelin.

THE HINDENBURG ONLINE

www.Hindenburg.net
This site gives a list of the passengers and crew. It also discusses theories about the cause of the fire.

www.archive.org/movies/details-db.php?collection=prelinger&collectionid=hindenberg_explodes
At this site, you can see photographs and newsreel clips of the *Hindenburg* disaster. Also included are shots of the airship over New York City.

FURTHER RESEARCH

If you are interested in finding out more, try researching the following topics on the Internet or at your local library:

- The element hydrogen and why it is so dangerous
- Nazi leader Adolf Hitler's rise to power in Germany
- The history of zeppelins.

INDEX